Nita Mehta's
Lebanese
Cooking

Nita Mehta

B.Sc. (Home Science), M.Sc. (Food and Nutrition), Gold Medalist

SNAB

Nita Mehta's
Lebanese
Cooking

ISBN 81-7869-159-0

Exclusive Distributor:

AMPRODUCTIONS
DIVISION OF: INFORMATION SCIENCE INDUSTRIES (CANADA) LIMITED

1169 Parisien St., Ottawa, Ont., K1B 4W4,
Tel: 613.745.3098 Fax: 613.745.7533
e-mail: amproductions@rogers.com
web: www.amproductions.ca

Published by:

SNAB
Publishers Pvt. Ltd.
3A/3 Asaf Ali Road,
New Delhi - 110002
Tel: 23252948, 23250091
Telefax:91-11-23250091
INDIA

Editorial and Marketing office:
E-159, Greater Kailash-II, N.Delhi-48
Fax:91-11-29225218, 29229558
Tel:91-11-29214011, 29218727, 29218574
E-Mail: nitamehta@email.com, nitamehta@nitamehta.com
*Website:*http://www.nitamehta.com
Website: http://www.snabindia.com

Printed at:

PRESSTECH LITHO PVT LTD, NEW DELHI

Price: $ 5.95

Contents

mezze (appetizers/dips)   7

chicken, meat & fish   26

rice & bread   36

vegetables   19

desserts   42

INTRODUCTION

*L*ebanon is a small country hugging the shores of the eastern Mediterranean. It has been a crossroads of cultures since recorded history began. Lebanese cuisine is one of the most interesting in the Mediterranean region. It combines the sophistication and subtleties of European cuisines with the exotic ingredients of the Middle and Far East.

Traditional food is based on local produce – olive oil, vegetables, grains, fruit and pulses. Beans and lentils, including the ever-present chickpeas, are an essential part of their diet. Lamb and chicken are preferred to mutton or beef. Many kinds of kebabs form a part of their famous mezze which is a varied and vast collection of appetisers.

For flavouring the Lebanese use an interesting mix of spices and herbs from both the East and the West. The main herbs used are fresh mint, parsley, and thyme. Spices include cinnamon, cumin, nutmeg and coriander.

Lebanese food appeals to the Indian palate because it uses many familiar ingredients. This is one cuisine that does not involve the mastering of complicated culinary techniques. The dishes are simple to make, fresh and colourful, aromatic and flavourful – superbly delicious!

Nita Mehta

INTERNATIONAL CONVERSION GUIDE

These are not exact equivalents; they've been rounded-off to make measuring easier.

WEIGHTS & MEASURES

METRIC	IMPERIAL
15 g	½ oz
30 g	1 oz
60 g	2 oz
90 g	3 oz
125 g	4 oz (¼ lb)
155 g	5 oz
185 g	6 oz
220 g	7 oz
250 g	8 oz (½ lb)
280 g	9 oz
315 g	10 oz
345 g	11 oz
375 g	12 oz (¾ lb)
410 g	13 oz
440 g	14 oz
470 g	15 oz
500 g	16 oz (1 lb)
750 g	24 oz (1½ lb)
1 kg	30 oz (2 lb)

LIQUID MEASURES

METRIC	IMPERIAL
30 ml	1 fluid oz
60 ml	2 fluid oz
100 ml	3 fluid oz
125 ml	4 fluid oz
150 ml	5 fluid oz (¼ pint/1 gill)
190 ml	6 fluid oz
250 ml	8 fluid oz
300 ml	10 fluid oz (½ pint)
500 ml	16 fluid oz
600 ml	20 fluid oz (1 pint)
1000 ml	1¾ pints

CUPS & SPOON MEASURES

METRIC	IMPERIAL
1 ml	¼ tsp
2 ml	½ tsp
5 ml	1 tsp
15 ml	1 tbsp
60 ml	¼ cup
125 ml	½ cup
250 ml	1 cup

HELPFUL MEASURES

METRIC	IMPERIAL
3 mm	1/8 in
6 mm	¼ in
1 cm	½ in
2 cm	¾ in
2.5 cm	1 in
5 cm	2 in
6 cm	2½ in
8 cm	3 in
10 cm	4 in
13 cm	5 in
15 cm	6 in
18 cm	7 in
20 cm	8 in
23 cm	9 in
25 cm	10 in
28 cm	11 in
30 cm	12 in (1ft)

HOW TO MEASURE

When using the graduated metric measuring cups, it is important to shake the dry ingredients loosely into the required cup. Do not tap the cup on the table, or pack the ingredients into the cup unless otherwise directed. Level top of cup with a knife. When using graduated metric measuring spoons, level top of spoon with a knife. When measuring liquids in the jug, place jug on a flat surface, check for accuracy at eye level.

OVEN TEMPERATURE

These oven temperatures are only a guide. Always check the manufacturer's manual.

	°C (Celsius)	°F (Fahrenheit)	Gas Mark
Very low	120	250	1
Low	150	300	2
Moderately low	160	325	3
Moderate	180	350	4
Moderately high	190	375	5
High	200	400	6
Very high	230	450	7

Lebanese Ingredients

Some special ingredients used in Lebanese cooking that may sound exotic, are either known to us by another name or have readily available substitutes.

BULGUR: Bulgur is a grain that is used frequently in Lebanese food. And its use is not restricted to the cereal section of the meal. It appears on the Lebanese diet in various forms - right from giving texture to Kibbeh to adding exotic taste to Tabulleh.

 Bulgur is made by parboiling the wheat, drying it, coarsely grinding it, removing the outer layers of the bran, and then cracking the grains. In India we call cracked wheat cereal *dalia*. Use wheat *dalia* in recipes asking for bulgur.

SUMAC: Sumac is a popular Middle Eastern spice. It is used to enhance the taste of salads and kebabs. Sumac looks like coarse paprika but has a lemony flavour. It is made from crushed and ground dried sumac berries. Though it is difficult to substitute this spice exactly but lemon juice serves well.

Lebanese Spice Powder

This dry powder is used in all the Lebanese recipes. Make extra & store. Use as needed. Increase quantity to double which makes grinding easier ! Store the excess.

Makes 4 tsp

INGREDIENTS

1 tsp black pepper corns (*saboot kali mirch*)
8-10 cloves (*laung*)
½ tsp nutmeg (*jaiphal*) - grated
½ tsp fenugreek seeds (*methi daana*)
½ tsp ginger powder (*sonth*)
1 tsp green cardamom seeds (*choti elaichi ke daane*)
1 tsp fennel (*saunf*)
2 star anise (*phool chakri*)
2" stick cinnamon (*dalchini*)

METHOD

1 Grind all the ingredients in a small mixer to a powder or crush with a pestle and mortar to a powder.

2 Store in a jar with a tight fitting lid and use as required. It lasts upto six months easily.

Mezze
(Appetizers/Dips)

Any Middle
Eastern restaurant
you go to or cookbook you
pick up has an extensive section
on mezze. So, what exactly is the mezze?
Mezze are often described as 'appetizers'. Similar
to the tapas of Spain & antipasto of Italy, mezze is an array
of little tidbits often served at the beginning of the meal. But mezze
are much more than mere appetizers, a mezze table can be the entire
dinner too. The dishes chosen for a mezze offer just the right contrast
of textures, aromas and flavours - Hot & cold, highly spiced and
barely spiced, sweet & sour. The most basic mezze will contain
Hummus bi Taheeni, Lebneh, a variety of olives & pickles
& bread. Or it may become an entire meal consisting
of grilled marinated seafood, skewered meats,
stuffed vine leaves & a variety of cooked
and raw salads.

Falafel

These world-famous fritters are served across the Middle East either tucked inside the pocket of a pita bread or as an appetiser. The main ingredient is no big secret – it is our very own chickpeas (kabuli channa)!

Serves 4

INGREDIENTS

½ cup dry chickpeas (*kabuli channa*)
½ onion - roughly chopped
1 flake garlic - crushed
1½ tbsp finely chopped fresh parsley or coriander/cilantro leaves
1 tsp ground coriander (*dhania powder*)
1 tsp ground cumin (*jeera powder*)
¼ tsp turmeric powder (*haldi powder*)
¼ tsp red chilli powder
¼ tsp black pepper (*kali mirch*) powder
1 tsp salt, or to taste
2 tbsp semolina (*suji*)
½ tsp baking soda (*mitha* soda)
oil for frying

METHOD

1 Soak the chickpeas overnight. Drain and place in the mixer.

2 Add the onions, garlic, fresh coriander/cilantro leaves, ground coriander, cumin, turmeric, red chilli powder, black pepper powder and salt. Grind to make a fine paste.

3 Add the semolina and baking soda. Mix well. Make small round balls, flatten them slightly.

4 Heat oil for frying in a wok. Fry 3-4 falafels at a time on medium heat till brown and cooked from inside.

5 Remove and drain on a paper towel. Repeat with the remaining falafels. Cook 2-3 minutes. Serve hot with hummus.

Note: *1½ tsp curry powder can be used instead of cumin, coriander, turmeric and chilli powder.*

Hummus (Chickpea Dip)

Hummus is often your first introduction to Middle Eastern food. This rich sauce is making an appearance at cocktail parties as a dip served with crackers. It is an essential part of a mezze platter served with Arabic bread, Kibbeh or Falafel.

Serves 4

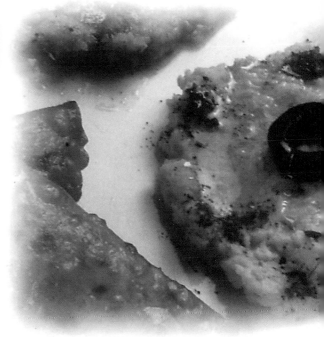

INGREDIENTS

2 tbsp dried chickpeas (*kabuli channa*) - boiled (½ cup) or ½ cup canned chick peas - drained
3 tbsp lemon juice
½ tbsp sesame seeds (*til*)
4 tbsp olive oil
1 tsp garlic paste
a pinch of black pepper powder
¼ tsp salt, or to taste

METHOD

1   Soak chickpeas overnight. Boil till cooked. Cool, drain and set aside.

2   Heat a nonstick pan/skillet. Add sesame seeds and toast, shaking frequently, until fragrant but not brown. Remove from heat and cool.

3   Place toasted sesame seeds and ½ tablespoon olive oil in the grinder and grind to a paste.

4   Add the chickpeas, lemon juice and garlic. Blend again until smooth.

5   With the machine running, add 2 tablespoon olive oil, a little at a time. Season with salt and pepper.

6   Spoon the hummus in the centre of a large platter. Drizzle with the remaining olive oil. Serve.

Note: *May be it is difficult to boil such a small quantity of chickpeas, I suggest you could boil extra and make fried chick peas as well. (given on page 12).*

9

Shish Taouk (Chicken Tikkas)

The marinade of yogurt, ginger-garlic and spices makes the chicken juicy, tender and full of flavour – these delicious morsels are grilled in the oven.

Serves 3-4

2 Add chicken pieces and onion. Keep aside covered for at least 4 hours in the fridge.

3 Preheat the oven at 180°C/350°F for 10 minutes.

INGREDIENTS

250 g/8 oz boneless chicken - cut into ¾" pieces
1 onion - cut into 8 pieces (½ cup)

MARINADE
1 egg, ½ tsp ginger-garlic paste
4 tbsp yogurt
½ tsp pepper, 1 tsp salt
1 onion - grated
1 tsp dried thyme or oregano
1 tsp Lebanese spice powder (pg 6)
1 tsp ground roasted cumin (*bhuna jeera*)
½ tsp red chilli powder or paprika powder (*degi mirch*)
2 tsp tomato ketchup
2 tsp lemon juice, 2 tbsp oil

4 Grease the wire rack with oil. Place the chicken pieces on it. Bake at 180°C/350°F in a preheated oven for 25-30 minutes or until the chicken is well cooked. Serve with tahini dip. (Pg 28)

METHOD

1 Mix all the ingredients of the marinade in a bowl.

Mini Vegetable Sambousik (Samosa)

The dough for sambousik has cornstarch and sugar which makes them different to samosa, but a close cousin nevertheless. Make a lightly spiced paneer filling or for a non-vegetarian version see Note below.

Makes 10

INGREDIENTS

¼ cup cornstarch
¾ cup flour (*maida*)
½ tsp salt, ½ tsp sugar
1 tbsp oil, ½ cup water

FILLING
60 g/2 oz grated paneer/tofu
¼ cup finely chopped fresh parsley or coriander/cilantro
¼ tsp red chilli powder
¼ tsp salt, 2 tbsp chopped onion
¼ tsp Lebanese spice powder (pg 6)

METHOD

1 Mix all ingredients of the dough. Add enough water to make a firm dough. Knead dough well. Cover and leave aside for 1 hour.

2 For the filling, mix all the ingredients of the filling and keep aside.

3 Divide dough into small lemon sized balls. Roll out to form circles (2-3" diameter). Cut the circle with a rour cookie cutter to get crinkled edges

4 Put filling on one side of circle. Fold over one end to make semicircles. Press edges with fingers so that they stick together. Use a little water for sticking.

5 Deep fry in hot oil over medium heat till golden brown on both sides. Serve hot.

Note: *For non-vegetarian version make the filling with 60 g/2 oz veg fine mutton mince (keema) in place of paneer/tofu and proceed in the same way.*

Fried Chickpeas

Chickpeas are used extensively in Lebanese cooking. Here boiled chickpeas are deep-fried then tossed with spices to make a tasty mint-flavoured nibble.

Serves 6-8

INGREDIENTS

1½ cups dried chickpeas (*kabuli channa*)
1 tsp salt, or to taste
1 tsp red chilli powder
2 tsp dried mint (*sookha poodina*) -
roasted & crushed
oil for frying

METHOD

1   Soak the chickpeas overnight.

2   Boil them with enough water to cover till cooked. Do not make them too soft and mushy. Drain well. Dry them on a kitchen towel.

3   Heat oil in a wok & deep fry the chickpeas in batches on medium heat, till they turn crisp.

4   Drain from oil and immediately sprinkle salt, chilli powder and mint while the chickpeas are still hot. Toss well to coat. Let them cool. Serve.

Note: *Canned chickpeas can be drained and used. Spread them out on a tray under the fan for them to dry out well, before frying.*

Kibbeh (Stuffed Mutton Balls)

The national dish of Lebanon is kibbeh. Mince and bulgur (dalia) are ground together then shaped into balls, stuffed with a filling of cooked mince and pinenuts and then deep-fried.

Serves 8

INGREDIENTS

1½ cups bulgur or *wheat dalia*
2 tbsp cornstarch, optional
700 g/1½ lb ground mutton (*keema*)
1½ cups roughly chopped onion
½ tsp Lebanese spice powder (pg 6)
3 tsp cumin powder (*jeera powder*)
2¼ tsp salt, 1½ tsp black pepper
oil for frying

STUFFING

225 g/7 oz ground mutton (*keema*)
¾ cup finely chopped onion
3 tbsp chopped pinenuts (*chilgoze*) or
peanuts - lightly toasted, ¾ tsp salt
1 tsp Lebanese spice powder (pg 6)

METHOD

1 Place bulgur or dalia in a bowl and cover with water. Soak for 20 minutes. Drain bulgur or dalia in a strainer, pressing to extract the excess liquid.

2 In a bowl mix together ground mutton, onions, Lebanese spice powder, cumin, salt, and pepper. Place in a mixer & grind to a paste.

3 Add the strained bulgur wheat and mix well. Grind again, in batches, until smooth and pliable enough to work like a dough, adding a little ice water if needed. If need be, add cornstarch for binding.

4 To make the stuffing cook the ground mutton over medium-high heat. Keep stirring, until meat is browned, about 4 minutes. Add the onions, pinenuts, salt and Lebanese spice powder. Cook, stirring, until tender, about 4 minutes. Keep aside to cool.

5 To make the kibbeh, shape the raw meat-bulgur mixture into egg-sized balls with oiled hands. Make a depression in the centre of a ball. Stuff the ball with about 1 tablespoon of the stuffing. Press down on the sides and top to enclose the filling. Reshape the meatball into a smooth egg with a pointed top.

6 Repeat with the remaining balls & stuffing, wetting your hands frequently.

7 Heat oil in a wok for deep frying. Add 4-5 kibbeh balls to the hot oil and cook until golden brown and the meat is cooked through, about 4 to 5 minutes. Remove with a slotted spoon and drain on paper towels. Serve hot.

13

Red Pepper & Walnut Dip

Walnuts and wheat crackers are ground to make the base of this popular dip. It is seasoned with grilled red pepper, green chilli and pomegranate juice. Serve it with kebabs, grilled meat and fish or as a tasty spread on toast.

Serves 4

INGREDIENTS

1 red pepper
1 green chilli
2 tbsp crumbled wheat crackers or dried bread crumbs
½ cup walnuts - roughly chopped
1 tsp lemon juice
2 tbsp pomegranate juice, fresh or ready-made or water
a pinch of ground cumin powder (*jeera*)
a pinch of sugar
¼ tsp salt, or to taste
2 tbsp olive oil

3 Peel off the blackened skin. Cut the pepper into 4 pieces and remove the seeds.

4 In a mixer add the crackers, walnuts, lemon juice, pomegranate juice, cumin, sugar, the roasted red pepper, roasted chilli and salt. Blend to a paste.

METHOD

1 Roast the red bell pepper and chilli over open flame (gas burner) until they are blistered, about 8 minutes. Alternately, put them under a grill (broil).

2 Place in a bowl and cover and keep aside for 10 minutes to sweat and loosen the skin.

5 With the machine running, add the olive oil in a thin stream. Mix well.

6 Serve as a dip with toasted pita wedges or with any snack.

Fattoush (Toasted Bread Salad)

Crunchy pieces of toasted pita bread are added to a wonderful mix of fresh garden vegetables tossed in a basic oil and lemon juice dressing.

Serves 6

INGREDIENTS

1 pita bread (7" in diameter)
½ cucumber - cut into small cubes without peeling (1 cup)
½ cup shredded lettuce
2 tbsp finely chopped parsley (optional)
2 tomatoes - cut into ½" pieces
4 green onions - chopped with the white portion
1 tbsp finely chopped fresh mint (*poodina*), 1 tbsp finely chopped fresh coriander/cilantro

DRESSING

2-3 flakes of garlic - crushed (1 tsp)
½ cup virgin olive oil
½ tsp salt
a pinch of black pepper powder
3 tbsp lemon juice

METHOD

3 To make the dressing, whisk all the ingredients together in a bowl, until it blends well.

1 Preheat the oven to 180°C /350°F. Split the bread in half through the centre and bake on a baking tray for 15 minutes, or until golden and crisp

4 Mix all the salad vegetables and add half of the dressing.

5 Add bread at serving time. Pour the remaining dressing. Toss to mix. Serve.

2 Break the pita bread into pieces.

Veg Mezze Platter

A typical mezze platter has deep-fried hot starters, fresh salads and dips with bread.

Serves 2

INGREDIENTS

1 pita bread or 1 pizza base
4 falafels (pg 8)
4 tbsp hummus dip (pg 9)
4 vegetable samosas (pg 11)
some fattoush (pg 15)
some tabulleh salad (pg 16)
Arabic pickle - recipe given below

METHOD

1 Make all the recipes as given on their respective pages.

2 Put 2 hot falafel cutlets and 2 hot samosas in the centre of the platter.

3 Put hummus dip on the right side and arrange salads on the other side of the platter. Arrange pickle on a cabbage or lettuce leaf.

4 Warm pita bread on a hot griddle, turning sides. Cut into 6-8 triangular pieces and serve separately on the side.

Mixed Arabic Pickle

Serves 4

INGREDIENTS

¼ cup peeled carrot - cut into thick sticks
¼ cup cucumber - cut into fingers with the peel
½ cup small cauliflower florets with little stalk
3 large flakes of garlic - sliced
1 onion - cut into 8 pieces
1 tbsp olive oil
¼ cup vinegar, 1 cup water
½ tsp salt, ½ tsp sugar

METHOD

1 Mix 1 cup water, vinegar, salt, and sugar in a pan. Bring to a boil. Remove from heat.

2 Add all the vegetables and olive oil. Mix and keep aside for 2 hours.

3 Store in an air tight glass jar. It lasts upto a month in the fridge. Use as required.

Tabulleh with a Twist

Tabulleh ranks along with Kibbeh and Hummus as the most popular of Lebanese dishes. Here it has been given a tasty twist with cooked minced chicken added to the traditional bright green and red mix of fresh herbs and vegetables.

Serves 4

METHOD

1 Place the bulgur in a large bowl and pour in enough hot water to cover generously. Let it stand until the grains soften, about 15 minutes.

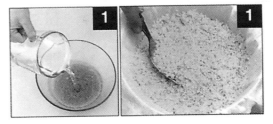

2 Drain well in a fine mesh strainer, pressing out excess water. Set aside.

3 In a frying pan, heat 2 tbsp oil over medium-high heat. Add the chicken mince. Cook, stirring, until no longer pink, about 4 minutes. Add cumin, salt, pepper, and cinnamon. Cook, stirring, for half a minute.

4 Add the onions. Saute until soft, about 3 minutes. Add the pinenuts (chilgoze) and cook until lightly roasted. Remove from the heat and let it cool slightly.

5 Place the mince mixture into a bowl. Add the bulgur and the remaining ingredients. Toss to combine. Adjust the seasoning to taste. Serve.

INGREDIENTS

½ cup bulgur or cracked wheat (*dalia*)
2 tbsp oil
100 g/3 oz ground chicken (*keema*)
½ tsp ground cumin (*jeera powder*)
¼ tsp salt, ½ tsp black pepper
½ tsp cinnamon powder (*dalchini*)
½ cup minced onions
¼ cup pine nuts (*chilgoze*) or walnuts
½ cup finely chopped tomatoes
½ cup finely chopped cucumber
¼ cup finely chopped parsley or coriander/cilantro
¼ cup finely chopped mint leaves (*poodina*)
¼ cup finely chopped green onions
2½ tbsp lemon juice
2½ tbsp olive oil

Vegetables

Garlic Stuffed Eggplant

Since eggplant is one of the most popular vegetables in Middle Eastern cuisine it has as many variations in cooking as the number of cooks! This version is tangy, tart & garlicky.

Serves 5

INGREDIENTS

5 long, thin eggplants (brinjals)
15 flakes of garlic
¼ cup pomegranate juice
1 tbsp ready-made tomato puree
½-¾ tsp salt, or to taste
¼ tsp black pepper powder
½ tsp sugar
¼ tsp cinnamon powder (*dalchini powder*)
¼ cup water
oil for frying

METHOD

1 Using a peeler, take off the peel from the brinjals, leaving alternate strips of peel on the vegetable.

4 Lay the fried brinjals side by side in a flat pan with a lid. Add pomegranate juice, tomato puree, salt, pepper, sugar, cinnamon and water. Keep on low heat for 5 minutes till soft and the liquid dries out. Remove from heat. Serve.

2 With a pointed knife, pierce each brinjal in three places and insert a clove of garlic in each incision.

3 Heat oil for frying. Deep fry the brinjals on medium heat, until soft and brown.

Paneer Shawarma Roll

An exciting new choice for shawarma lovers – soaking the paneer fingers in the marinade gives them a strong flavour.

Serves 4

INGREDIENTS

250 g/8 oz *paneer* or tofu - cut into 2"
long fingers
1 tomato - sliced, 1 small onion - sliced
2 pita breads or pizza bases - cut into
two pieces horizontally to get 2 thin
rounds
some hummus (pg 9)
some arabic pickle (pg 16)
2 tbsp oil

MARINADE
1 tsp lemon juice or vinegar
1 tsp Lebanese mixed spices (pg 6)
¼ cup thick yogurt
¼ tsp ground cardamom (*choti elaichi*)
1 tbsp oil, ½ tsp ginger-garlic paste
1 tsp salt, ½ tsp pepper, or to taste

METHOD

1 Marinate paneer/tofu with all the ingredients of the marinade for about ½ hour. You can keep it longer if you feel like.

2 Heat 2 tbsp oil in a pan, add paneer/tofu fingers and stir fry for 3-4 minutes or till slightly golden brown from some sides. Remove from heat.

3 Warm all the four pieces of pita bread on a hot griddle/pan for 1 minute. Keep one warmed piece on a flat surface. Spread 1 tsp hummus, put some paneer/tofu slices. Top it with sliced tomatoes and onion. Roll forward to make a roll. Serve along with Arabic pickle.

Grilled Vegetable Kabobs

Colourful diced veggies and cubed paneer are soaked in a marinade to tickle the taste buds. Put them on bamboo skewers and grill lightly – who could ask for more!

Serves 4

INGREDIENTS

250 g/8 oz cauliflower - separated into ½"
florets
200 g/6 oz mushrooms - keep whole, if
small or cut into 2" pieces
200 g/6 oz tofu or paneer - cut into 1"
pieces
2 onions - cut into 1" pieces
1 red bell pepper - cut into 1" pieces
1 yellow bell pepper - cut into 1" pieces
1 green bell pepper - cut into 1" pieces

MARINADE
½ cup olive oil, 2 tbsp lemon juice
½ cup finely chopped coriander/cilantro
leaves
1 tsp dried marjoram or oregano
1 tbsp ground cumin seeds (*jeera powder*)
1 tsp dry ginger (*sonth*)
1 tsp salt, 1 tsp black pepper powder
1 tbsp paprika (*degi mirch*)

METHOD

1 Combine all the marinade ingredients. Mix all vegetables except cauliflower to the marinade. Set aside.

2 Boil water in a saucepan. Add the cauliflower and boil for 3-4 minutes or till crisp-tender. Remove cauliflower from hot water and drain through a sieve. Pat dry.

3 Add the blanched cauliflower to the marinated vegetables in the bowl.

4 Cover and refrigerate for at least 30 minutes or up to 4 hours, stirring occasionally.

5 Thread the marinated vegetables on skewers. Reserve the marinade for basting.

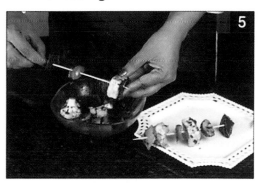

6 Grill the vegetables in a hot oven, rotating the skewers occasionally. Baste the vegetables several times with the reserved marinade. Grill until vegetables are cooked and lightly browned.

7 Serve hot sprinkled with cumin powder and lemon juice.

Mushrooms in Lebanese Spices

Mushrooms were unknown in classical Arab cuisine but are now being introduced into the diet. Typical Lebanese herbs and spices transform mushrooms into memories of the Arabian nights.

Serves 4

INGREDIENTS

400 g/12 oz mushrooms - thickly sliced
¾" stick cinnamon (*dalchini*)
½ tsp cloves (*laung*)
1½ tsp coriander seeds (*saboot dhania*)
3 tbsp olive oil
1½ tbsp lemon juice, 1 tsp oregano
2 tsp chopped fresh parsley or coriander/cilantro
2 tsp chopped fresh mint leaves (*poodina*)
¼ tsp salt, or to taste
¼ tsp black pepper powder

METHOD

1 Crush cinnamon, clove and coriander seeds in a mortar and pestle.

2 Heat 3 tbsp oil in a frying pan. Add the mushrooms and 1 tsp of freshly ground spices. Cook for 1- 2 minutes, stirring occasionally. (Store the remaining spice mixture).

3 Stir in lemon juice, the herbs, salt and pepper. Cook for 1 more minute. Serve hot.

Spinach & Chickpeas

Chickpeas and spinach create a wonderful partnership of contrasting textures in this earthy and healthy dish.

Serves 4

INGREDIENTS

4 cups chopped spinach
2 cups diced tomatoes
½ cup chickpeas (*kabuli channas*) -
boiled or 1 cup canned chick peas-
drained
3 tbsp oil
1 onion - sliced
2-4 flakes garlic - minced (1 tsp)
1 tsp ground coriander (*dhania powder*)
salt to taste
¼ tsp red chilli powder or flakes

METHOD

1 Soak chickpeas overnight.

2 Place them in a deep pan with enough water to cover. Cook till done. Keep aside along with the cooking liquid.

3 Heat oil in a nonstick frying pan/ skillet. Add the onions and garlic. Cook until the onion is soft. Add the salt and spices.

4 Add the spinach. Cook, stirring, till the spinach turns soft and the water dries. Add chickpeas and some of the cooking liquid, to make some gravy. Mix well.

5 Add the tomatoes. Cook for 10-15 minutes. Check salt and remove from heat. Serve hot.

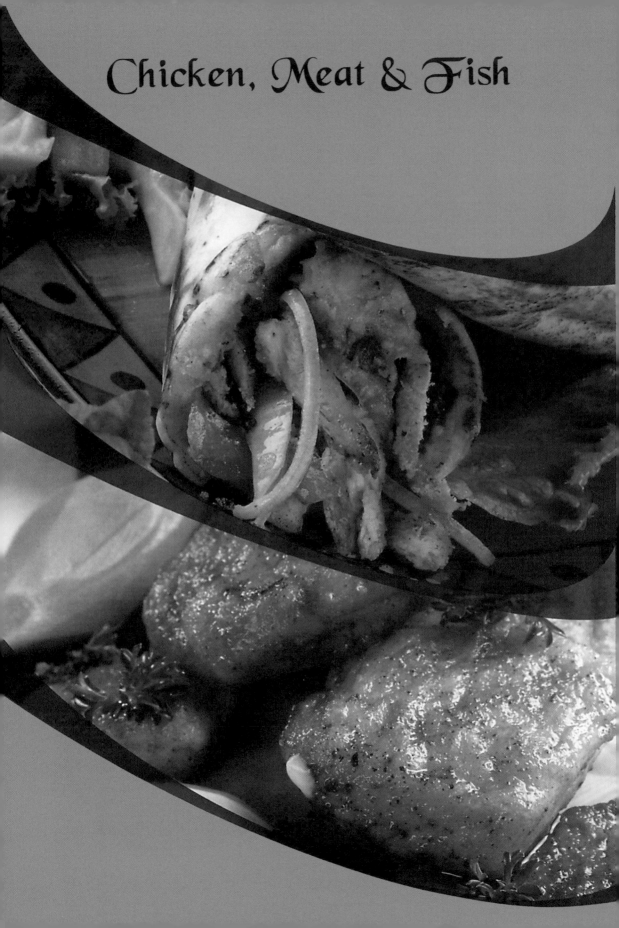

Chicken, Meat & Fish

Cold Chicken with Walnut Sauce

The Arab world is full of examples of chicken flavoured with nut oils. Here is a version of cold chicken with a rich walnut sauce.

Serves 6

INGREDIENTS

500 g/1 lb boneless chicken - cut into
1" pieces
2 cups water
½ carrot - roughly chopped
½ cup roughly chopped onion
1 flake garlic - peeled and crushed
1 tbsp chopped fresh coriander/cilantro
or parsley
1 bay leaf (*tej patta*)
½ tsp black peppercorns, 1 tsp salt
¾ cup shelled walnuts
1½ slices white bread
½ tbsp paprika or *Kashmiri* red chillies

METHOD

1 Place the chicken, water, carrot, onion, garlic, parsley, bay leaf, peppercorns and salt in a large saucepan. Bring to a boil and simmer for 10 minutes or until the chicken is tender.

2 Let the chicken cool in the broth. Strain. Pick up the chicken pieces discarding the other ingredients and vegetables. Reserve the stock.

3 Dice the boiled chicken into ¼" pieces. Set aside.

4 Grind the walnuts, bread and paprika together in a mixer with the reserved stock to make a smooth paste.

5 Mix the diced chicken with the walnut paste. Place on a serving platter.

6 Sprinkle with some pepper.

Chicken Shawarma Roll

For today's generation a roll is the perfect meal-on-the-go. In this gourmet-class version marinated chicken is pan-fried then rolled up in pita bread that has been generously buttered with hummus.

Serves 2

INGREDIENTS

250 g/8 oz boneless chicken breast
2 pita breads or pizza bases - cut horizontally to get 2 thin rounds
some hummus or tahini dip
Arabic pickle (pg 16)

MARINADE

1 tsp lemon juice or vinegar
1 tsp Lebanese mixed spices (pg 6)
¼ tsp ground cardamom (*choti elaichi*)
¼ cup yogurt
1 tbsp oil, ½ tsp ginger-garlic paste
½ of a well beaten egg
1 tsp salt, ½ tsp pepper, or to taste

1 tomato - sliced
1 small onion - sliced (½ cup)

METHOD

1 Slice the chicken into long pieces.

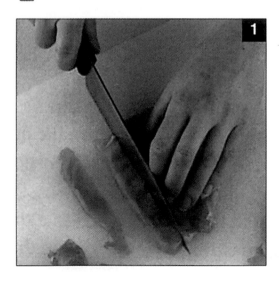

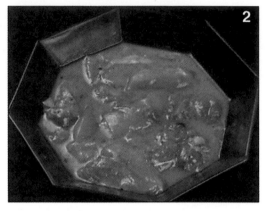

2 Mix all the ingredients of the marinade in a bowl. Add sliced chicken and keep aside for at least 4 hours or more in the fridge.

3 Heat 2 tbsp oil in a pan/skillet, add chicken along with the marinade. Stir fry for 4-5 minutes, till golden brown. Cook covered for 3-4 minutes or till tender.

4 Cut each pita bread horizontally into 2 pieces. Warm all the four pieces of pita bread on a hot pan/skillet for 8-10 seconds. Keep one warmed piece on a flat surface. Spread 1 tsp hummus or tahini paste, add chicken slices. Top it with sliced tomatoes and onion. Roll forward to make a roll. Serve with Arabic pickle.

Note: *Tahini is a thick paste made of ground sesame seeds and is available ready-made.*

Spice-coated Pan-fried Fish

This out-of-the-ordinary fried fish has a subtle coating of fragrant spices – ginger, cumin, cinnamon & cloves. As an extra bonus it is drenched in pomegranate juice or lemon juice.

Serves 4

INGREDIENTS

500 g/1 lb boneless fish - cut into fillets
4 tbsp any cooking oil, 2 tbsp olive oil
1 tsp red chilli powder or paprika
chopped fresh parsley or coriander/
cilantro
2 tbsp fresh pomegranate juice or
lemon juice

SEASONED FLOUR
½ cup flour *(maida)*, 2-3 peppercorns
¼ tsp ground ginger *(sonth)*
¼ tsp cumin seeds *(jeera)*
¼ tsp all spice powder (optional)
¼" cinnamon stick (dalchini)
2 cloves *(laung)*
½ tsp salt
¼ tsp nutmeg powder *(jaiphal)*

METHOD

1 In a mixer blend together all the ingredients for the seasoned flour. Remove to a plate.

2 Roll the fish fillets in seasoned flour to coat both sides, shaking to remove any excess flour.

3 In a nonstick frying pan/skillet, heat 4 tbsp oil. Add fish to the hot oil in batches and cook until golden brown for about 2 minutes per side shaking the pan to prevent the fish from sticking. Remove and drain on paper towels.

4 Heat the 2 tbsp olive oil in a separate pan. Add the red chilli powder or paprika. Cook for ½ a minute on low heat till the oil is infused with the chilli. Remove from heat. Add fried fish to this pan. Coat well.

5 To serve garnish the hot fish with parsley and drizzle with pomegranate or lemon juice.

Chicken with Onions

Boneless marinated chicken pieces & plenty of sliced onions are allowed to cook slowly in their own juices. Nutmeg, cinnamon, thyme & cumin add their magical charm.

Serves 8

INGREDIENTS

750 g/1½ lb boneless chicken - cut into
16-18 pieces
3 tbsp lemon juice
¼ tsp nutmeg powder
¼ tsp cinnamon powder
½ tsp black pepper ground, ½ tsp salt
6 tbsp olive oil
6 onions - sliced thinly
1 tsp ginger-garlic paste
8 tbsp yogurt
2 tsp salt
2 tsp dried thyme or oregano
2 tsp Lebanese spice powder (pg 6)
2 tsp ground roasted cumin (*bhuna jeera powder*)
1 tsp red chilli powder or paprika
4 tsp tomato ketchup

METHOD

1 Combine 1½ tablespoon lemon juice, nutmeg, cinnamon, pepper and salt.

2 Mix in the chicken pieces and marinate, refrigerated, for 4 hours or overnight.

3 Heat 6 tbsp oil in a wok. Add onions and cook till light golden.

4 Add chicken and cook over a medium heat, about 20 minutes, till chicken is done.

5 Add the remaining lemon juice, and all other remaining ingredients. Cook for 5 minutes. Serve hot.

Stuffed Potatoes with Laban Sauce

In the Lebanese kitchen all kinds of vegetables are hollowed out, stuffed, then baked. In this delicious recipe scooped potatoes are filled with cooked minced meat and walnuts, and layered with thick garlicky yogurt.

Serves 6-8

INGREDIENTS

300 g/10 oz mutton mince
4 potatoes
1/3 cup coarsely chopped walnuts
3 tbsp oil
1 onion - sliced thinly
½ tsp cinnamon
½ cup minced fresh parsley/coriander/cilantro

LEBAN SAUCE

2 cups yogurt
2 flakes of garlic - crushed
2½ tsp cornstarch
1½ tsp salt, a pinch black pepper

METHOD

1 Wash and scrub the potatoes well to remove all dirt. Dry and rub with oil. Prick the potatoes on all sides a few times with a fork.

2 Boil the potatoes till just done. While the boiled potatoes are still warm, halve them lengthwise.

3 Scoop out the inner portion very neatly, leaving ¼" border. Place the potato shells aside till baking time. Chop the scooped out potato coarsely. Keep aside for the filling.

4 For the sauce, in a small bowl dissolve the cornstarch in the yogurt. Place the yoghurt mixture in a saucepan and cook on low heat. Simmer for 5 minutes, stirring continuously. Add a pinch of black pepper powder. Stir in the garlic paste & salt into the cooking yogurt. Simmer the sauce, stirring occasionally, for 2 minutes. Keep aside.

5 For the filling, heat 3 tbsp oil in a pan. Add the walnuts. Cook over low heat, stirring, for 1-2 minutes, or until they are golden. Remove walnuts from the pan and keep aside.

6 To the oil remaining in the pan add the onion. Cook, stirring occasionally, until golden. Add the mince. Cook about 8-10 minutes, stirring frequently to break up the lumps. Remove from heat.

7 Combine together the walnuts, meat mixture, chopped potato, cinnamon, parsley, ½ teaspoon salt and a pinch of pepper. Fill the mixture in the potato shells.

8 Spread half of the sauce in a dish. Arrange the potato shells over it. Spoon the remaining yogurt sauce on top.

9 Bake the potatoes in a preheated oven at 230°C/450°F for 10 to 15 minutes.

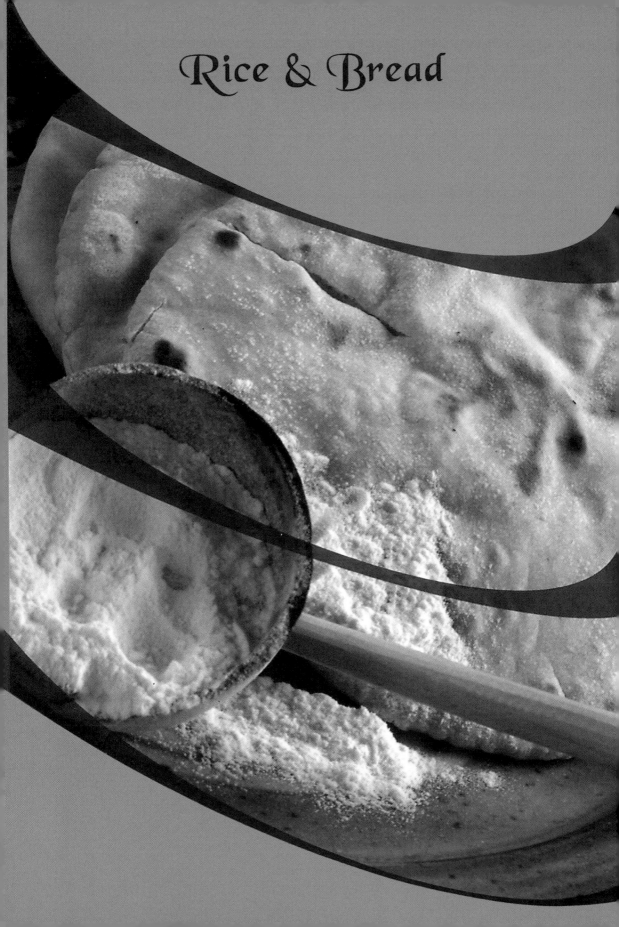

Zaatar Flat Bread

Bread is so highly regarded in the Middle East that in some Arabic dialects it is called 'esh' meaning 'life'. In Lebanon every meal includes some kind of bread, often seasoned with spices and oil or with a special spice blend called zaatar.

Serves 4

INGREDIENTS

1 tbsp dry yeast, 1 tsp sugar
1 cup lukewarm water
3 cups all-purpose flour
½ tsp salt, 6 tbsp olive oil

ZAATAR
2 tsp dried thyme or oregano
1 tsp dried marjoram or basil
2 tbsp finely chopped fresh coriander/cilantro
3 tbsp sesame seeds (*til*)

METHOD

1 Mix together ½ cup lukewarm water and sugar till the sugar is dissolved. Sprinkle the yeast on top.

2 Mix the yeast into the warm sugar-water mixture. Cover and keep in a warm place undisturbed, allowing it to dissolve.

3 After 5 or 10 minutes, the yeast should begin to form a creamy foam on the surface of the water. If there is no foam in the bowl, the yeast is dead and you should start again with a new packet of yeast.

4 In a large bowl, mix together the flour, the proved yeast and salt. Add some of the remaining water and knead into a firm dough. Use only as much water as required. Cover and leave to rise for 45 minutes or until dough has doubled in bulk. Punch down dough and transfer to a floured board and knead briefly.

5 Place the dough, covered, in the refrigerator for at least 2 hours or overnight. Bring the dough to room temperature before proceeding.

6 Mix together the ingredients for the zaatar. On a floured surface break the dough off into 10- 12 pieces. Form into balls.

7 On a well-floured surface roll out one ball of the dough. Stretch the dough to form an elongated shape. Brush the top of the bread with a little olive oil. Spread a little zaatar mixture on top.

8 Place the rolled bread on an oiled baking tray. Repeat with the rest of the dough balls. Bake for 7-8 minutes at 180°C/300°F, or till the bread is cooked.

Lentils with Bulgur Pilaf

This simple dish of lentils, grain and onions is a favourite in the Middle East. According to tradition, this is the food referred to in the Biblical account of Esau's great hunger when he sold his birthright as first born to his twin brother Jacob.

Serves 4

INGREDIENTS

1 cup green lentils (*sabut moong*)
3 cups water, 1 cup bulgur or *dalia*
¾ tsp salt, 3 tbsp olive oil
½ cup finely chopped onion
2 tsp minced garlic
1 tsp ground cumin seeds (*jeera*)
½ tsp ground cinnamon (*dalchini*)
¼ tsp black pepper powder
a pinch grated nutmeg (*jaiphal*)
pinch of all spice or a pinch clove
powder
1½ cups thinly sliced onions
¼ cup chopped parsley, for garnish

METHOD

1 In a medium pot, combine the lentils and water. Bring to a boil. Lower the heat, cover and simmer until lentils are almost done but still firm, 15 to 20 minutes.

2 Add the bulgur and ½ tsp salt. Remove from heat and cover. Let it sit until the bulgur is tender and the water is absorbed, 20 to 25 minutes, adding more water if the bulgur seems dry.

3 In a large pan, heat 2 tbsp oil over medium-high heat. Add the chopped onions. Cook, stirring, until very soft, 5 minutes.

4 Add the garlic, cumin, cinnamon, remaining ¼ tsp salt, black pepper, nutmeg and all spice. Cook, stirring, for 1 minute.

5 Stir in the lentil and bulgur mixture. Mix well to combine. Remove from heat. Set aside.

6 In a frying pan, heat the remaining oil over medium heat. Add the sliced onions.

7 Cook, stirring occasionally, until caramelized to a very rich brown colour, 10- 15 minutes.

8 Transfer the lentil and bulgur mixture to a serving bowl and top with the caramelized onions.

9 Sprinkle with chopped parsley.

Pita Bread

In this recipe pita bread is cooked on a griddle, just like a chappati. The detailed instructions teach you how to handle a yeast dough. Get set to become an expert pita maker!

Serves 4

INGREDIENTS

2 tsp dry yeast
2 cups plain flour (*maida*)
1½ cups whole wheat flour (*atta*)
½ cup lukewarm water, 1 tbsp sugar
1 cup water, or as needed
1 tbsp olive oil, ½ tsp salt

METHOD

1 Mix together ½ cup lukewarm water & sugar till the sugar is dissolved. Sprinkle the yeast on top. Mix the yeast into the warm sugar-water mixture. Cover & keep in a warm place undisturbed, allowing it to dissolve.

2 After 5 or 10 minutes, the yeast should begin to form a creamy foam on the surface of the water. If there is no foam in the bowl, the yeast is dead and you should start again with a new packet of yeast.

3 In a large bowl mix together the flours, the proved yeast, oil and salt. Mix well to combine all ingredients. Knead to form a dough. Remove dough to a large oiled bowl. Cover and leave to rise for 45 minutes or until dough has doubled in size.

4 Punch down dough and transfer to a floured board and knead briefly. Place the dough, covered, in the refrigerator for at least 2 hours or overnight. Bring the dough to room temperature before proceeding.

5 Divide the dough into 8 pieces and form into balls. Use maida to flour your hands when working on the dough. On a well-floured surface, roll one ball of dough into an 8-inch circle (just like a chappati).

6 Heat the griddle. Place the rolled pita on the hot griddle. Cook for 15 to 20 seconds before turning the bread over gently. Cook for another minute or until big bubbles appear.

7 Turn the bread again. Use a kitchen cloth to press on those areas where bubbles have formed to push air into the flat areas. Cook until the pita balloons. Remove pita. Repeat with the remaining dough balls.

Semolina Flat Bread

You will be delighted to learn how to make these Middle Eastern chappatis using semolina (suji) instead of flour.

Serves 7

INGREDIENTS

2½ cups very fine semolina (*suji*)
¾ tsp salt, or to taste
6 tbsp olive oil

METHOD

1 Place semolina in a large bowl, stir in salt and 2 tbsp of olive oil.

2 Gradually add water and knead into a soft dough. Keep it aside covered for 15-20 minutes. If the dough becomes firm then add little water and knead again to get a soft dough.

3 Divide into 8 pieces. Form into balls, roll out a ball into a chappati.

4 Heat griddle over medium heat. Place the bread. Cook for a minute. Smear ½ tbsp oil. Turn side. Cook on both sides till golden patches appear on it. Repeat with the rest of the dough.

Note: *If you are using coarse semolina, grind it in the grinder once to get fine semolina.*

Desserts

Cardamom Yogurt Pudding with Nuts & Honey Syrup

Imported cardamom is highly prized in Middle Eastern cooking. Here it is used to gently scent a luscious & dreamy dessert which uses the local products – honey, figs & walnuts.

Serves 4

INGREDIENTS

2 cups yogurt, 6 tbsp sugar
1 tsp vanilla essence
½ tsp cardamom powder (*elaichi* powder)
¼ cup water, 2 tsp gelatine

SYRUP

¼ cup walnuts or ¼ cup almonds
12 dried figs (*anjeer*) - cut into four
¼ cup honey, ¼ cup water
2 tbsp lemon juice
1" cinnamon stick (*dalchini*)
1 tsp sugar

METHOD

1 Whisk together yogurt, sugar, vanilla and cardamom in a small bowl until sugar is dissolved.

2 In a small vessel, put ¼ cup water. Sprinkle gelatine on it and leave to soak for 5 minutes. Keep on very low heat and stir till gelatine dissolves.

3 Whisk a little yogurt gradually into the hot gelatine mixture. Add this to the remaining yogurt and mix well.

4 Pour yogurt mixture into 4 ramekins. Cover & chill, until set, about 1½ hours.

5 While yogurt is chilling, prepare the syrup. Heat a pan/skillet over medium heat. Add walnuts & almonds. Toast until they become fragrant. Remove and allow to cool. When cool enough to handle, chop the toasted nuts roughly. Keep aside.

6 Cook the figs, honey, water, lemon juice, cinnamon stick & sugar in the same pan Cook, over medium heat, for about 10 minutes until fruit is soft.

7 Remove from heat and let it cool. Remove the cinnamon stick.

8 Spoon the cooked fruit on to the set yogurt pudding. Sprinkle the toasted nuts on top. Serve immediately.

Cream-filled Apricots

A variety of dried fruits and nuts are an essential part of the cuisine of the Arab world.
This simple apricot pudding is an example of a rich heritage.

Serves 5

INGREDIENTS

10 pieces dried apricots (*khurmani*)
¼ cup sugar
1 tsp lemon juice
½ cup heavy whipping cream
4-5 almonds (*badam*) - chopped finely

GARNISH
finely slivered almonds & pistachios

METHOD

1 Soak apricots in warm water for 2 hours to soften. Drain. Cut each apricot with a sharp knife into 2 pieces.

2 In a saucepan mix sugar, lemon juice and 1 cup water. Bring to a boil and cook until sugar mixture is syrupy for about 5 minutes.

3 Add the apricots and simmer for 5 minutes. Remove from heat and allow to cool.

4 Whip cream with a beater until stiff peaks form.

5 Gently fold the finely chopped almonds into the cream.

6 In the serving dish arrange half the apricot pieces in a single layer. Dollop cream mixture onto the apricots.

7 Cover with the remaining apricots, like a sandwich. Garnish with almonds and pistachios.

Lebanese Cake

This cake has a chewy, dense texture and a delightful yellow colour which makes it different from ordinary cakes. Try it and see!

Serves 4

INGREDIENTS

1½ cups semolina (*suji*)
½ cup plain flour (*maida*)
½ tsp turmeric powder (*haldi*)
1½ tsp baking powder
1 cup sugar
1 cup milk
½ cup oil
1 tbsp pinenuts (*chilgoze*)

METHOD

1 Preheat oven to 180°C/350°F.

2 Grease a 7" baking tin.

3 Mix together semolina, flour, turmeric and baking powder in a bowl. Set aside.

4 In a big bowl combine milk and sugar. Stir until sugar is dissolved.

5 Add flour mixture & oil to the milk. Beat with an electric beater at medium speed for about 5 minutes.

6 Pour the batter into the prepared baking tin. Sprinkle pinenuts on top. Bake for 40 minutes, or until a wooden pick inserted in centre comes out clean. Let it cool in the oven for 5 minutes. Take out on a wire rack. Garsnish with powdered sugar and candied orange peel. Serve.

Glossary of Names/Terms

HINDI OR ENGLISH NAMES AS used in India	USED IN USA/UK/OTHER COUNTRIES Other countries
Aloo	Potatoes
Badaam	Almonds
Baingan	Eggplant, aubergine
Basmati rice	Fragrant Indian rice
Bhutta	Corn
Bhindi	Okra, ladys finger
Capsicum	Bell peppers
Chaawal, Chawal	Rice
Chickpeas	Garbanzo beans
Choti elaichi	Green cardamom
Chilli powder	Red chilli powder, Cayenne pepper
Cornflour	Cornstarch
Coriander, fresh	Cilantro
Cream	Heavy whipping cream
Dalchini	Cinnamon
French beans	Green beans
Gobhi	Cauliflower
Hara Dhania	Cilantro/fresh or green coriander leaves
Hari Gobhi	Broccoli
Hari Mirch	Green hot peppers, green chillies
Elaichi	Cardamom
Imli	Tamarind
Jeera Powder	Ground cumin seeds
Kadhai/Karahi	Wok
Kaju	Cashewnuts
Katori	Individual serving bowls resembling ramekins
Khumb	Mushrooms
Kishmish	Raisins
Kofta	Balls made from minced vegetables or meat, fried and put in a curry/gravy/sauce.
Maida	All purpose flour, Plain flour
Makai, Makki	Corn
Matar	Peas
Mitha soda	Baking soda
Nimbu	Lemon